1-2-3

Numbers and Counting Workbook

by Allison Hall

Quail Publishers

Quail Publishers

Published by
Quail Publishers L.L.C
info@quailpublishers.com
www.quailpublishers.com

The publisher grants teachers permission to photocopy pages from this book for classroom use only. No other part of this publication may be reproduced, stored in a retrieval system or transmitted in any form or by any means, electronic, mechanical, photocopying, recording or otherwise, without the prior permission of the publisher.
All verses are adaptations from the Authorized King James Version of The Holy Bible.

Written by Allison Hall
Cover and Interior design by Earl Roumell
Interior illustrations by Pete McDaniel and Earl Roumell
Education Consultant: Gertrude McKenzie
Editor: Keisha Hall

ISBN: 978-0-9894627-1-6

Copyright © 2014 by Allison Hall. All rights reserved
Printed in the U.S.A.

Contents

Introduction 4
Teaching with Bible Math: 1-2-3 5

Activity Sheets 1-10
One 6-7
Two 8-9
Three 10-11
Four 12-13
Five 14-15
Six 16-17
Seven 18-19
Eight 20-21
Nine 22-23
Ten 24-25
Activities for Numbers 1-10 26-29

Activity Sheets 11-20
Eleven 30-31
Twelve 32-33
Thirteen 34-35
Fourteen 36-37
Fifteen 38-39
Sixteen 40-41
Seventeen 42-43
Eighteen 44-45
Nineteen 46-47
Twenty 48-49
Activities for Numbers 11-20 50-51
Revision Exercise 52-55

INTRODUCTION

Children learn mathematical concepts every day in their environment. Many know, for instance, that most persons have two eyes, two ears and ten fingers on their bodies. Recognizing numerals, counting and computation are critical math skills which children should grasp at an early stage in their development. Bible Math: 1-2-3 is designed to help children master these concepts and skills. The book provides children with the opportunity to recognize numerals and number names, count, do simple computation and learn more about the Bible. This promotes early math skills and Bible knowledge. The book is also fully integrated to the early childhood and children's Bible study curriculums.

The book is divided into two sections. In the first section, there are simplified Bible verses to help children better understand mathematical concepts in an integrated manner. For example:

Five smooth stones for a war
With a giant from a far. **1 Samuel 17:40**

In the second section, numbers eleven to twenty are taught using objects that are mentioned in the Bible.

When children participate in the activities they will:

- Recognize numerals and number names
- Form numerals correctly
- Count in sequence
- Distinguish between numerals that look similar to each other
- Conduct simple computation, such as addition and subtraction

TEACHING WITH BIBLE MATH: 1-2-3

How to use the activity sheets

1. Review the numeral you will be teaching.
2. Read the story relating to each simplified Bible verse.
3. Develop an exciting and engaging lesson which allows for multisensory activities.
4. Make sure that children have the necessary stationery and resources to participate in the lesson.
5. Read the instructions to children.
6. Use manipulatives, songs, poems, or tell the Bible story relating to each image or simplified verse, to make the lesson exciting.
7. Use the activity sheets to teach the formation of each numeral, as well as for computation tasks. Make sure that you demonstrate the proper pencil grip and sequence in which each numeral is formed.
8. Make sure that homework is family centered and allows children to use resources in their homes or communities.

Play and Learn

Invite children to do a variety of movements that teach "how many". For example, you can clap two times; then ask them how many times you clapped your hands. You can also have them race to collect a selected number of objects from a group. Ask them to say the number of objects they have collected.

Suggested Songs

Use songs, poems and nursery rhymes, to help you to teach children how to count. Below is a list of some great songs to make your lesson exciting. You can access the lyrics and rhythm of these songs on the Internet and on our website.

- ♪ Animals went in two by two
- ♪ One, Two, Buckle My Shoe
- ♪ 1, 2, 3, 4, 5, Jesus is alive
- ♪ Five Little Ducks
- ♪ Ten Green Bottles standing on the Wall
- ♪ Children go where I send thee
- ♪ Ten Little Indians

Name _____

1 one

Trace the numbers. Then write some on your own.

₁
↓ | ┆ ┆ ┆ ┆ ┆

Trace the number names. Then write some on your own.

one one one

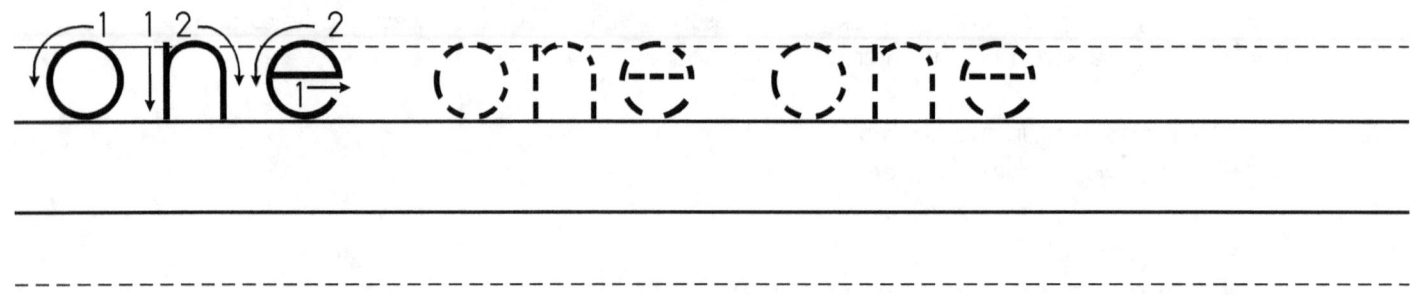

One bright sun rules the day
and shows God's love in every way.   **Psalm 136:8**

Name _____

Trace the numbers. Then write some on your own.

Draw and color **1** sun in the sky.

Count the **suns**. Then place a circle around **1** of them.

Name _____

2
two

Trace the numbers. Then write some on your own.

2 2 2 2 2

Trace the number names. Then write some on your own.

two two two

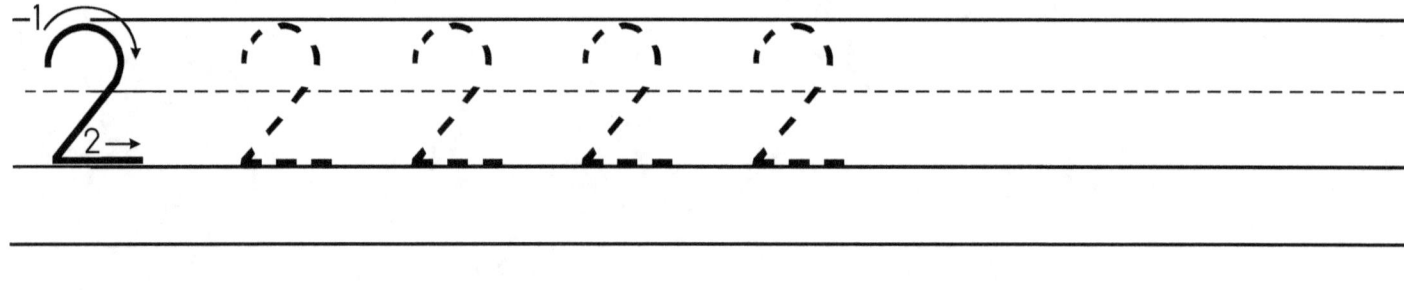

Two dogs went into the ark
soon the sky became very dark. **Genesis 7:9**

Name _____

Trace the numbers. Then write some on your own.

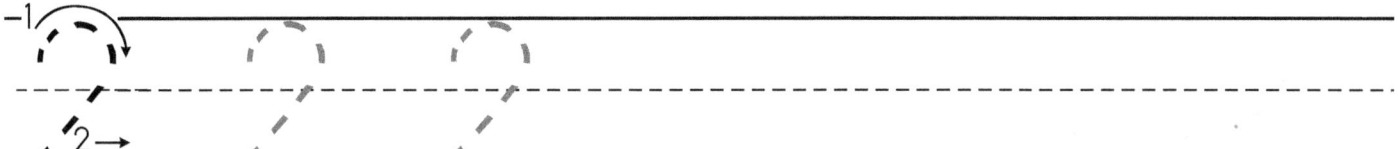

Draw and color **2** eggs in the nest.

Count the **dogs**. Then place circles around **2** of them.

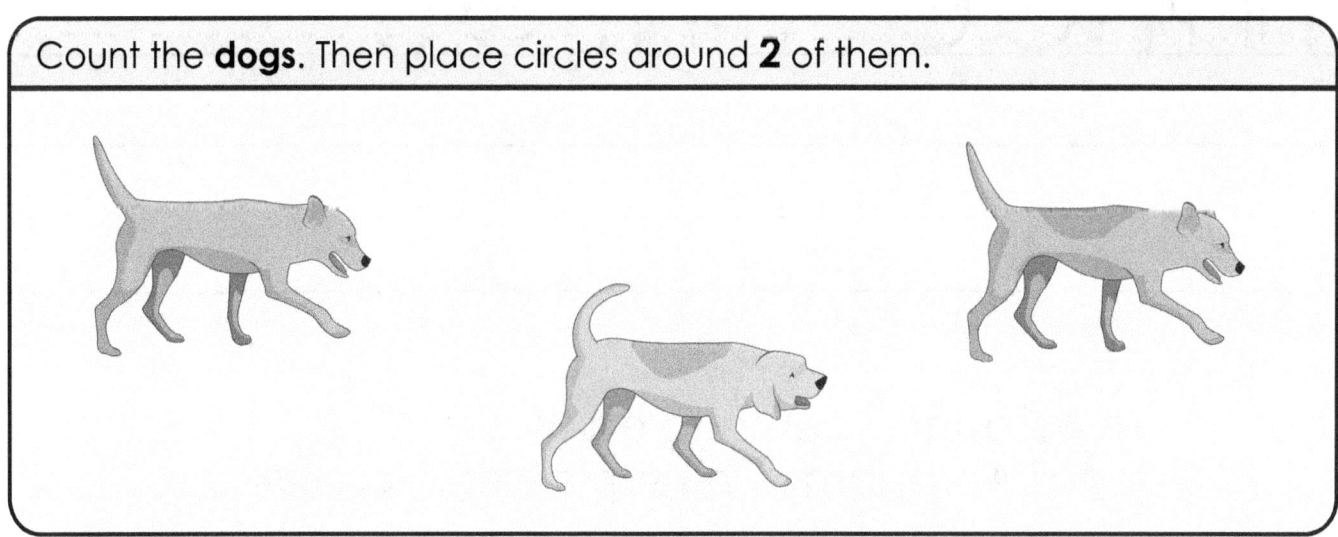

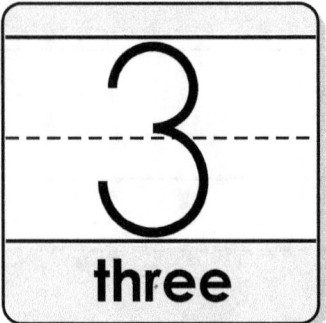

Name _____

Trace the numbers. Then write some on your own.

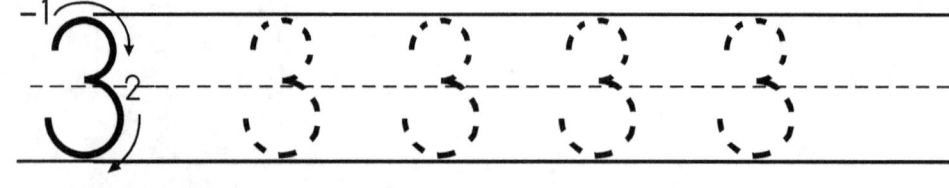

Trace the number name. Then write some on your own.

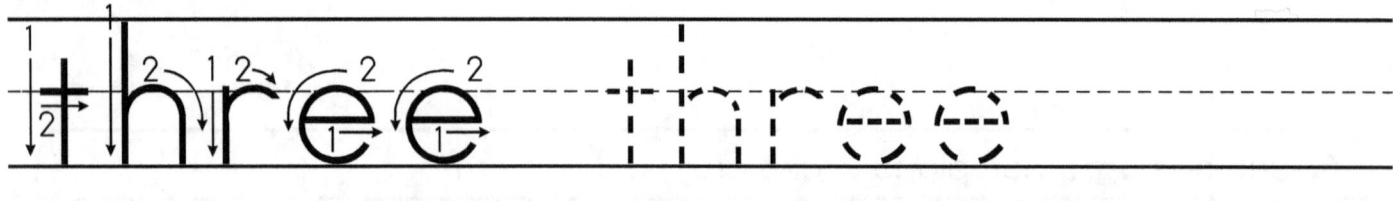

Three angels came to earth
to tell Abraham of his son's birth.   **Genesis 18:2**

Name _____

Trace the numbers. Then write some on your own.

3 3 3

Draw and color **3** crosses on the hill. ✝

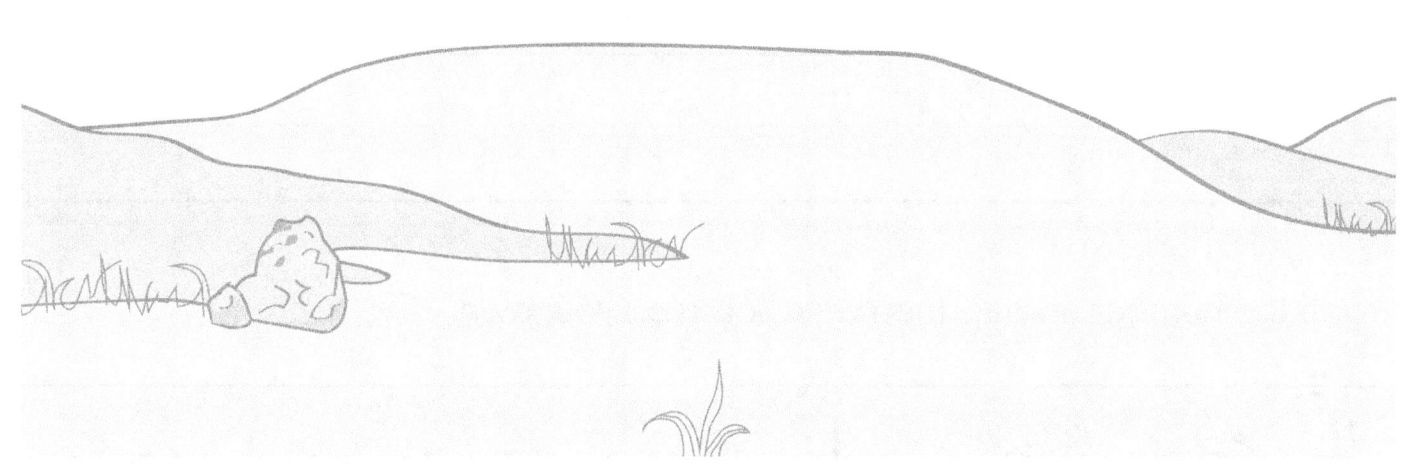

Count the **angels**. Then place circles around **3** of them.

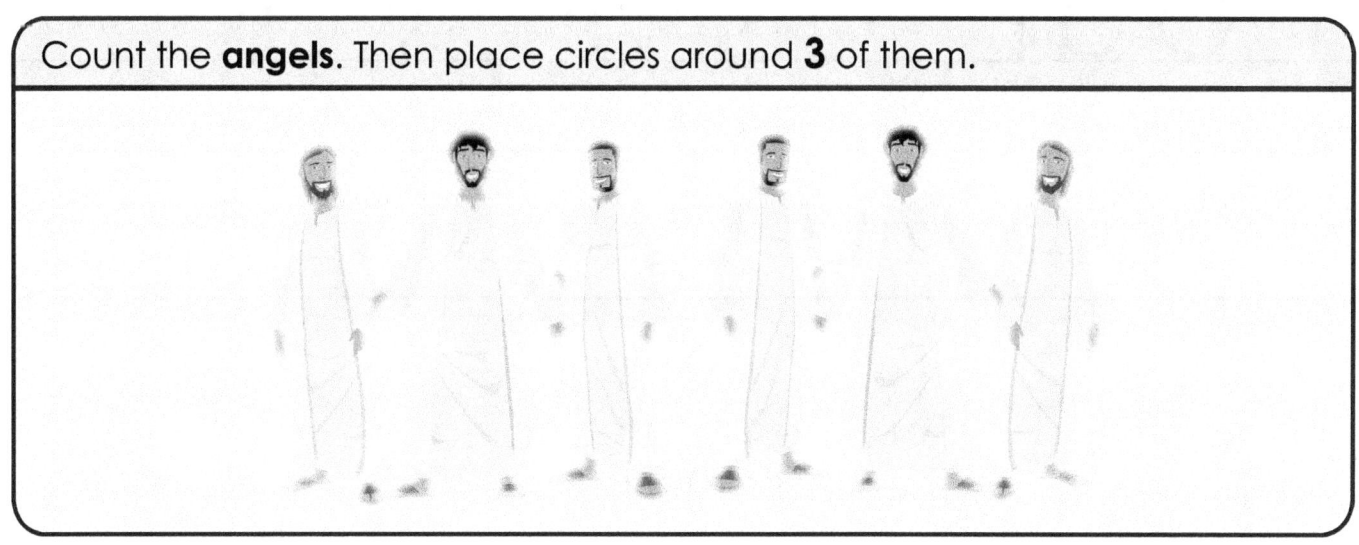

Quail Publishers L.L.C Bible Math:1-2-3 Activity Sheets 11

Name _____

four

Trace the numbers. Then write some on your own.

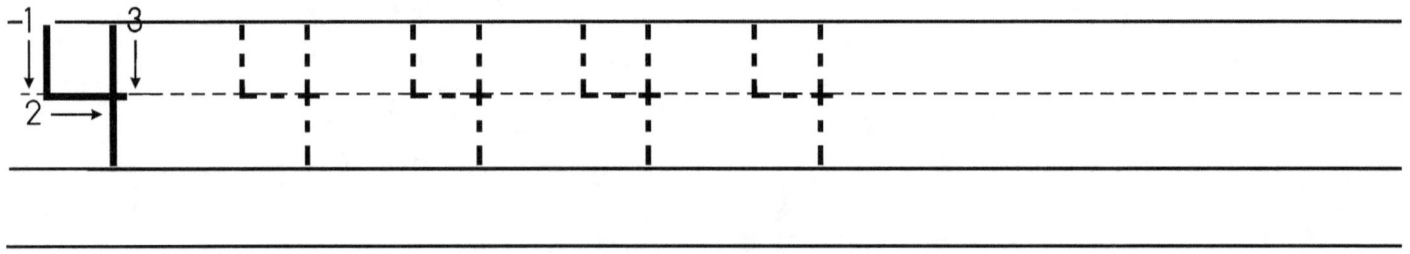

Trace the number names. Then write some on your own.

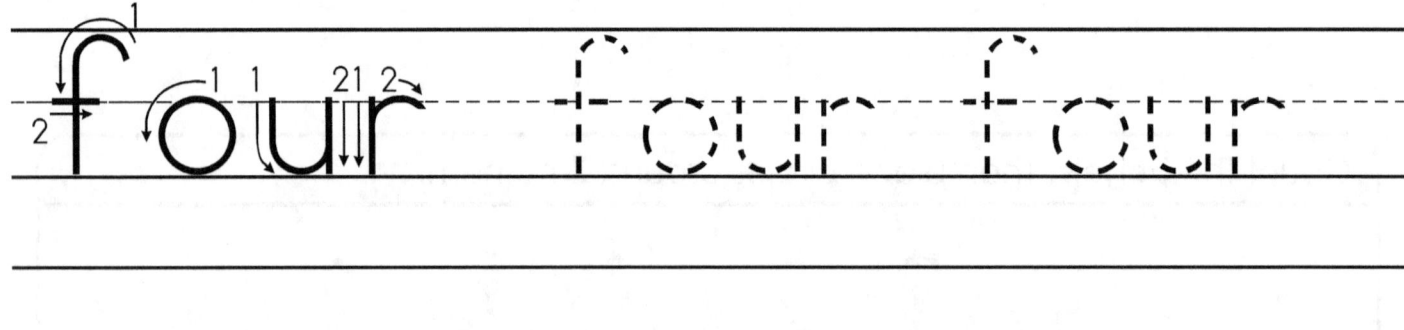

Four men refused to eat the king's meat. **Daniel 1**

Name _____

Trace the numbers. Then write some on your own.

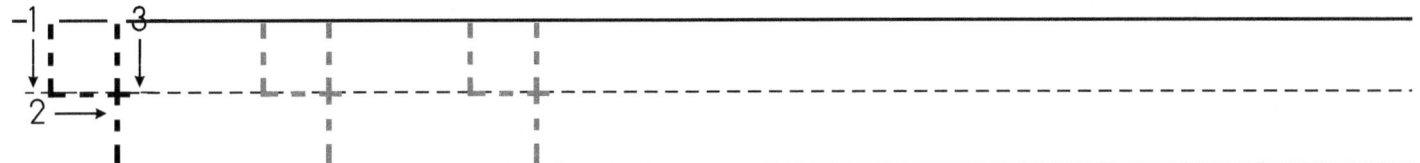

Draw and color **4** cookies in the plate.

Count the **men**. Then place circles around **4** of them.

Quail Publishers L.L.C

Name _____

5 five

Trace the numbers. Then write some on your own.

5 5 5 5 5

Trace the number names. Then write some on your own.

five five five

Five smooth stones for a war
with a giant from a far.   **1 Samuel 17:40**

Name _____

Trace the numbers. Then write some on your own.

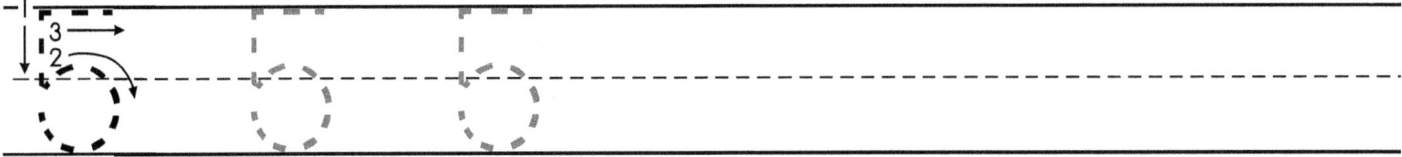

Draw and color **5** candles on the cake.

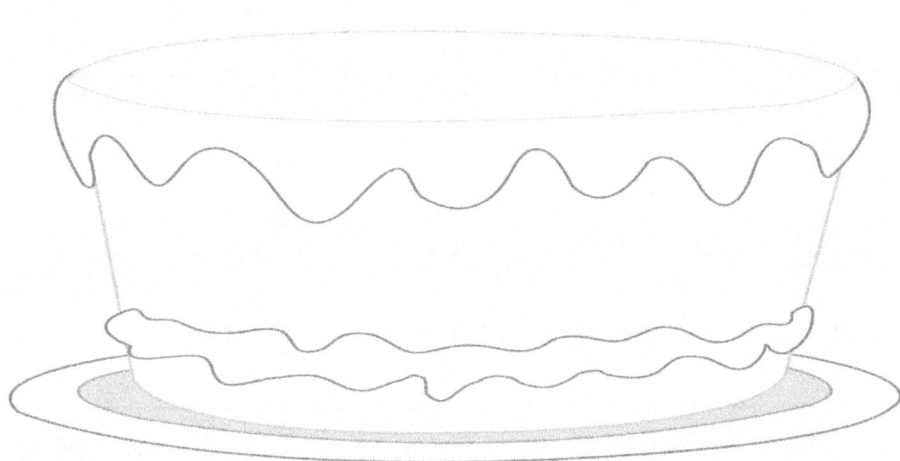

Count the **stones**. Then place circles around **5** of them.

Quail Publishers L.L.C

Name _____

6
six

Trace the numbers. Then write some on your own.

6 6 6 6 6

Trace the number names. Then write some on your own.

six six six six

Six jars of water turned into wine
served all the guests just fine. John 2:1-9

16 Bible Math: 1-2-3 Activity Sheets

Quail Publishers L.L.C

Name _____

Trace the numbers. Then write some on your own.

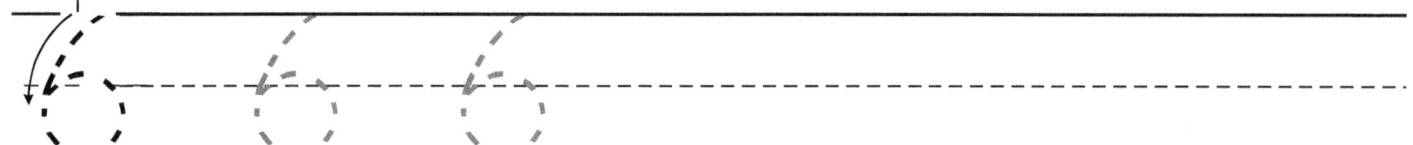

Draw and color **6** balloons.

Count the **jars**. Then place circles around **6** of them.

7 seven

Name _____

Trace the numbers. Then write some on your own.

Trace the number name. Then write some on your own.

Seven lambs were used to tell that Abraham had dug a well. **Genesis 21:28-30**

Bible Math: 1-2-3 Activity Sheets

Quail Publishers L.L.C

Name _____

Trace the numbers. Then write some on your own.

Draw and color **7** apples on the tree.

Count the **lambs**. Then place circles around **7** of them.

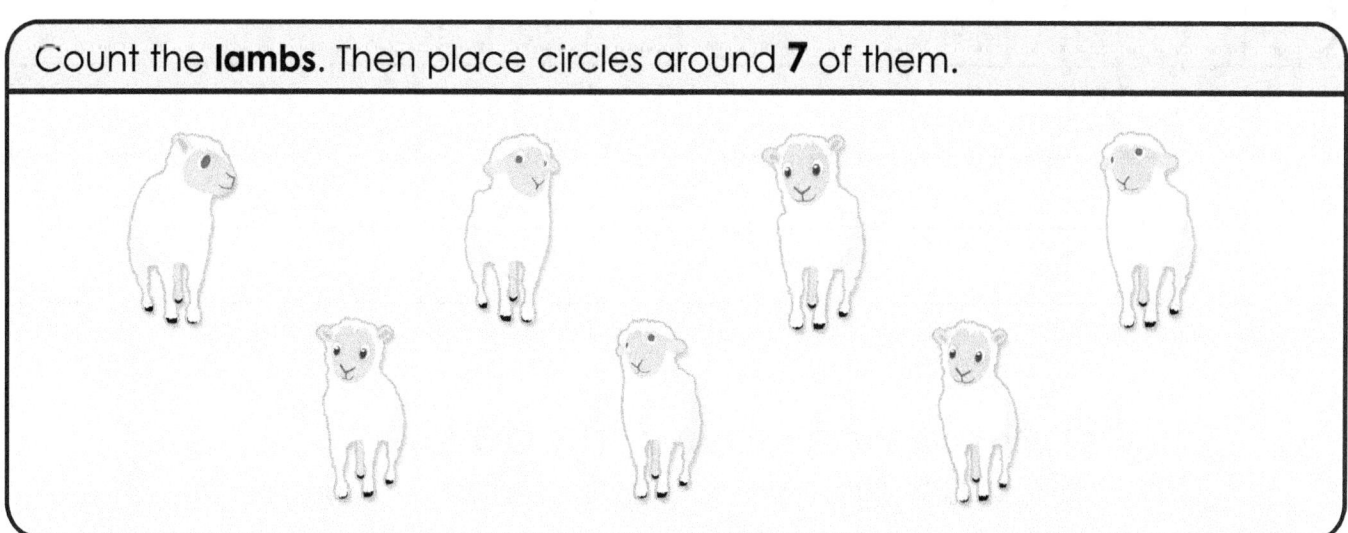

Quail Publishers L.L.C

Bible Math: 1-2-3 Activity Sheets 19

Name _____

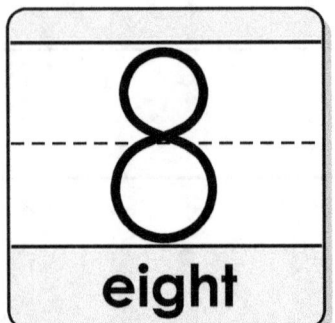

Trace the numbers. Then write some on your own.

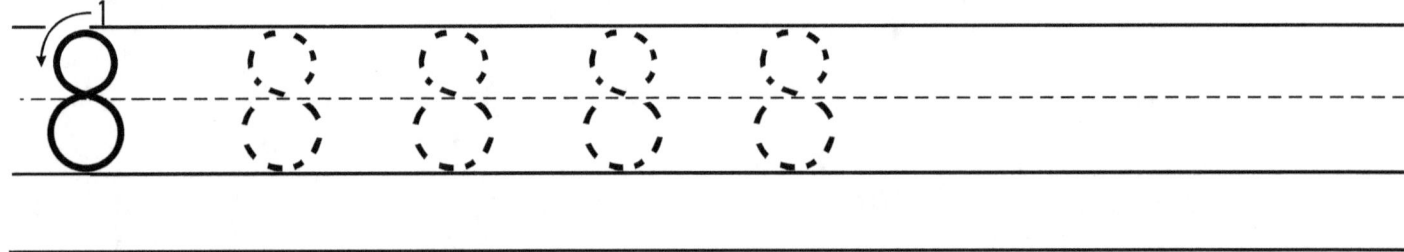

Trace the number name. Then write some on your own.

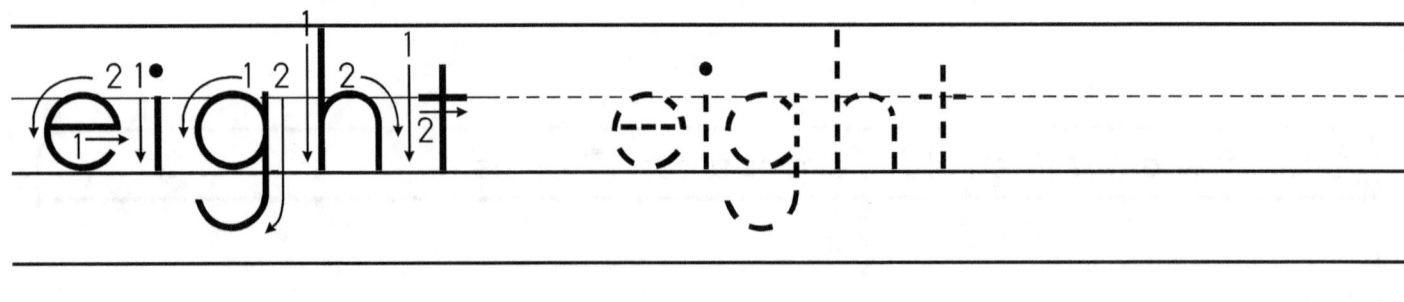

Eight people were saved the day
the rain washed everything away . Genesis 7:13

Name _____

Trace the numbers. Then write some on your own.

Draw and color **8** cones of ice cream for a treat.

Count the **persons**. Then place circles around **8** of them.

Quail Publishers L.L.C

Bible Math: 1-2-3 Activity Sheets

Name _____

9
nine

Trace the numbers. Then write some on your own.

9 9 9 9 9

Trace the number names. Then write some on your own.

nine nine nine

Nine lepers did not say,
"Thank you Jesus for saving the day."   Luke 17:17

Name_____

Trace the numbers. Then write some on your own.

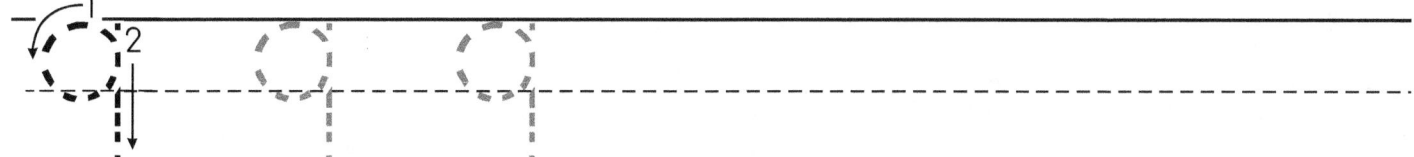

Draw and color **9** lollipops. 🍭

Count the **lepers**. Then place circles around **9** of them.

Name _____

Trace the numbers. Then write some on your own.

Trace the number names. Then write some on your own.

Ten coins are safe and sound
when the lost coin was found. Luke 15:8-10

Name _____

Trace the numbers. Then write some on your own.

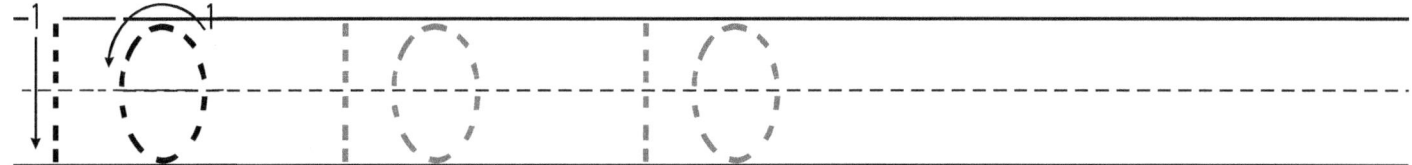

Draw and color **10** coins to buy a gift. 1¢

Count the **coins**. Then place circles around **10** of them.

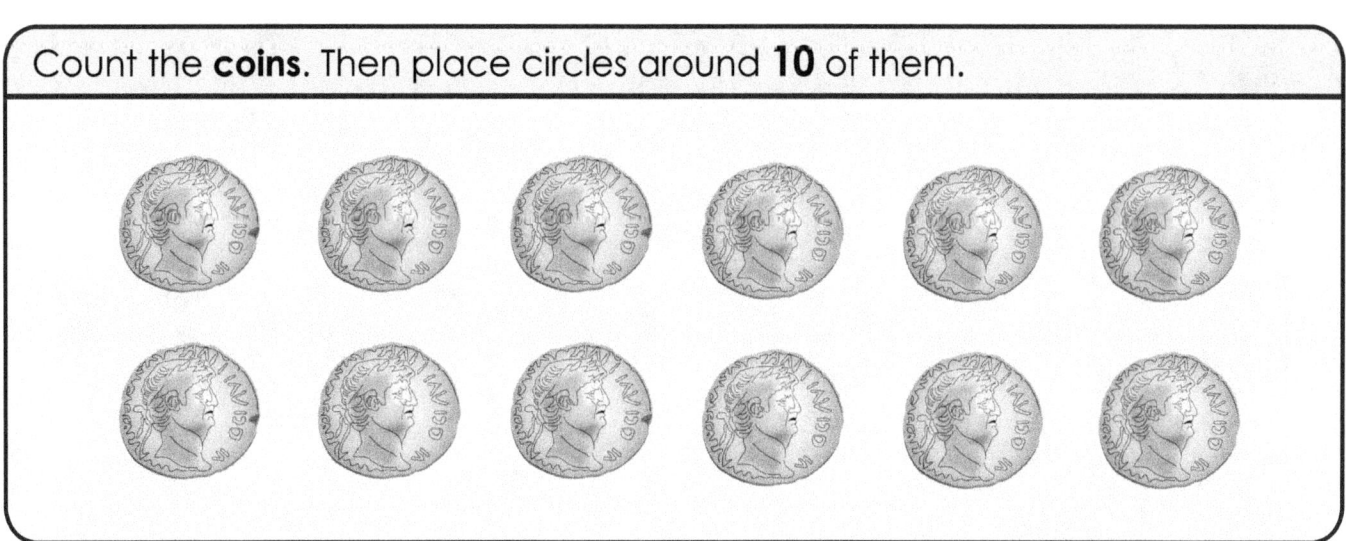

Name_____

Draw a line to match the numbers to the correct groups.

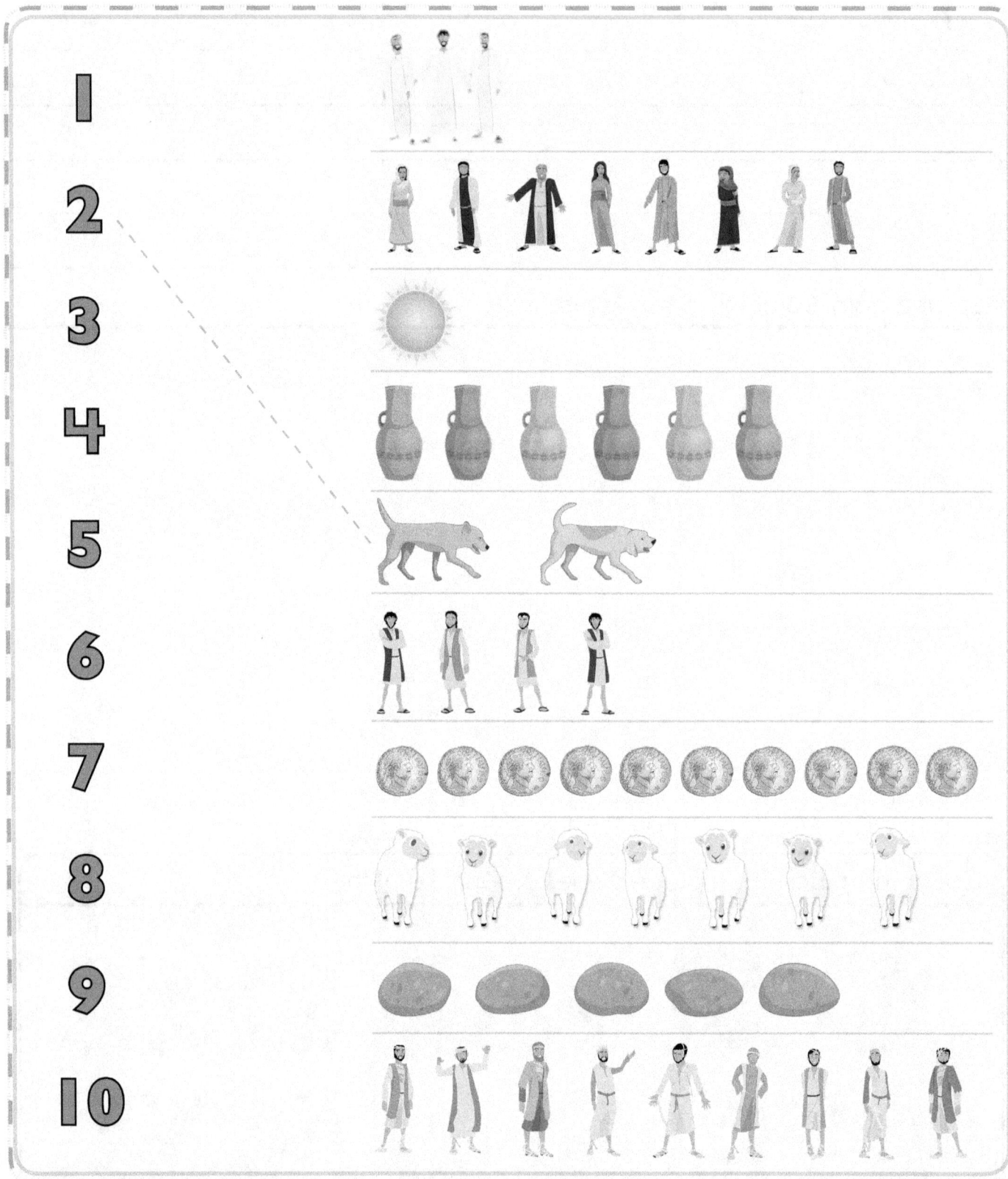

Name _____

Circle the numbers that represent the number names.

One	9	5	3	(1)
Two	2	4	6	3
Three	6	4	3	5
Four	5	2	3	4
Five	3	5	7	9
Six	9	6	8	5
Seven	8	6	7	4
Eight	9	10	8	7
Nine	6	9	7	8
Ten	10	8	2	9

Write the missing numbers in the empty spaces below to complete the table.

1		3		5
6		8		10

Write the correct number names in the empty spaces below to complete the table.

one	three		five
six	eight		ten

Quail Publishers L.L.C

Bible Math: 1-2-3 Activity Sheets

Name _____

ADDITION

When we add, we put things together. The plus or addition sign (**+**) is used to show that we are adding things. **Add** the following groups.

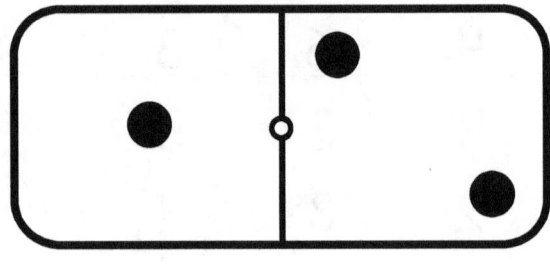

1 + 2 =

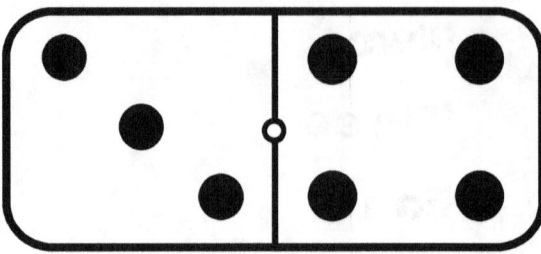

3 + 4 =

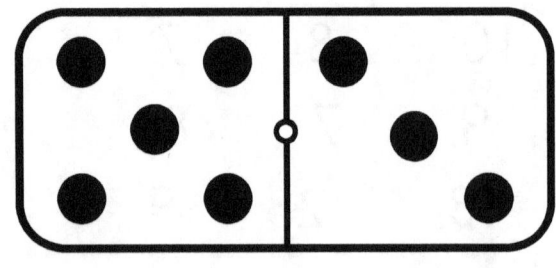

5 + 3 =

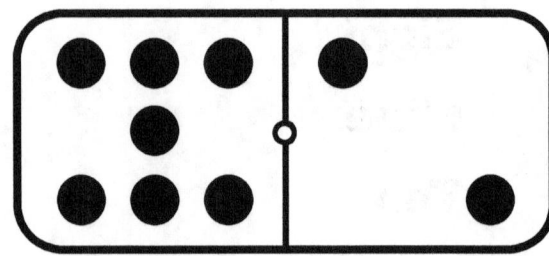

7 + 2 =

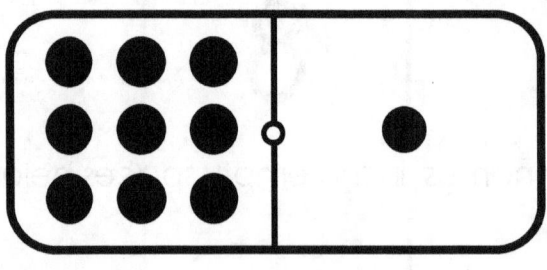

9 + 1 =

Name_____

SUBTRACTION

When we subtract, we take things away from a group. The minus or subtraction sign (−) is used to show that we are doing subtraction. Cross out the objects to show that you are **subtracting** and to help you to get the answer.

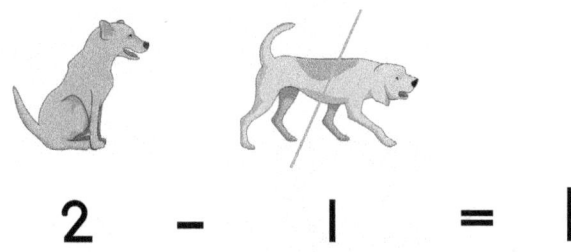

2 − 1 = 1

4 − 3 =

7 − 5 =

9 − 6 =

10 − 8 =

Name _____

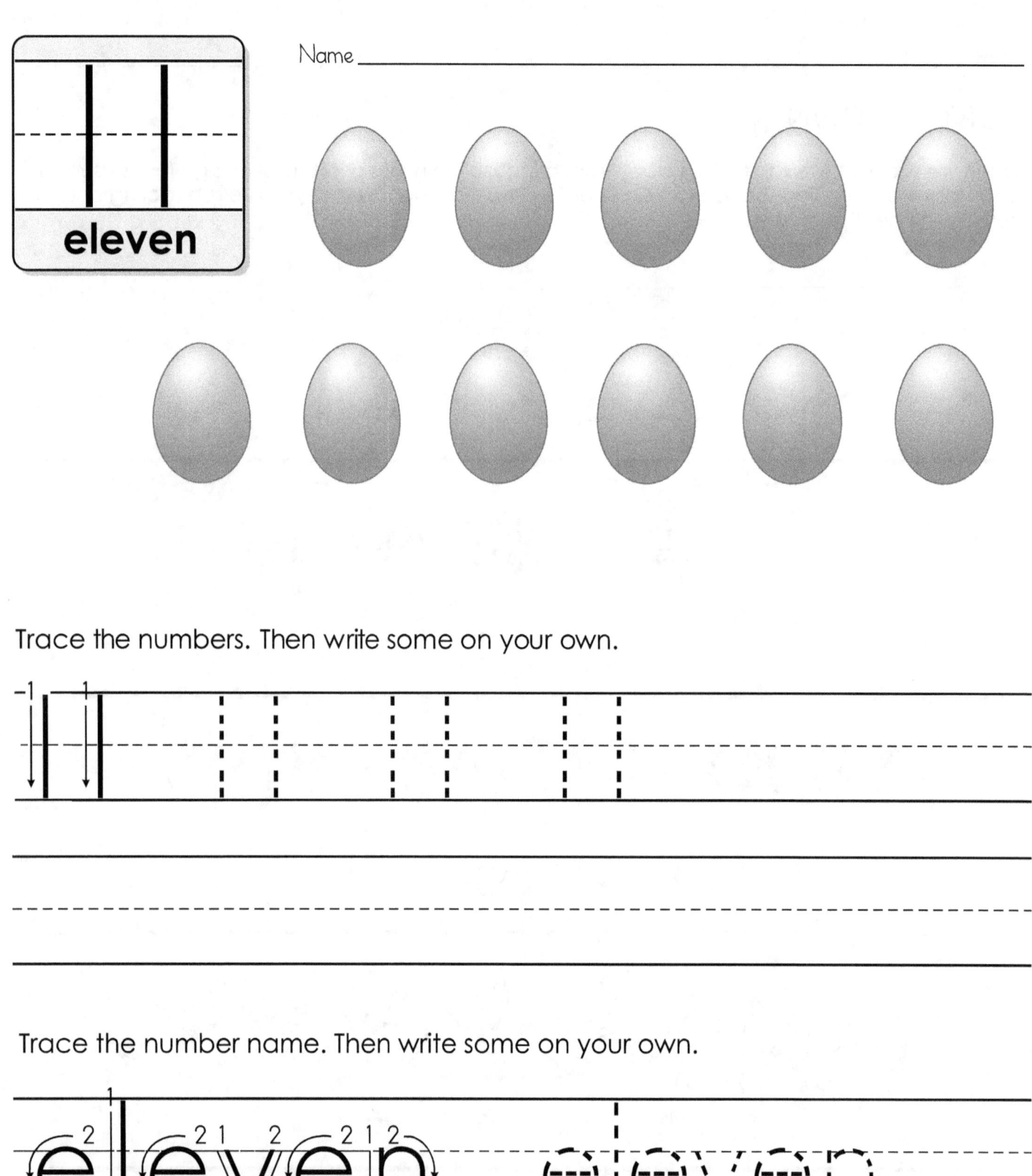

Trace the numbers. Then write some on your own.

Trace the number name. Then write some on your own.

Bible Math: 1-2-3 Activity Sheets

Quail Publishers L.L.C

Name _____

Trace the numbers. Then write some on your own.

Draw **1** more circle. Then count how many circles there are in all.

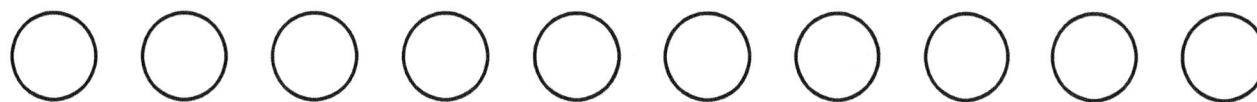

There are _____ circles.

Count the **eggs**. Then place circles around **11** of them.

Quail Publishers L.L.C   Bible Math:1-2-3 Activity Sheets

Name _____

Trace the numbers. Then write some on your own.

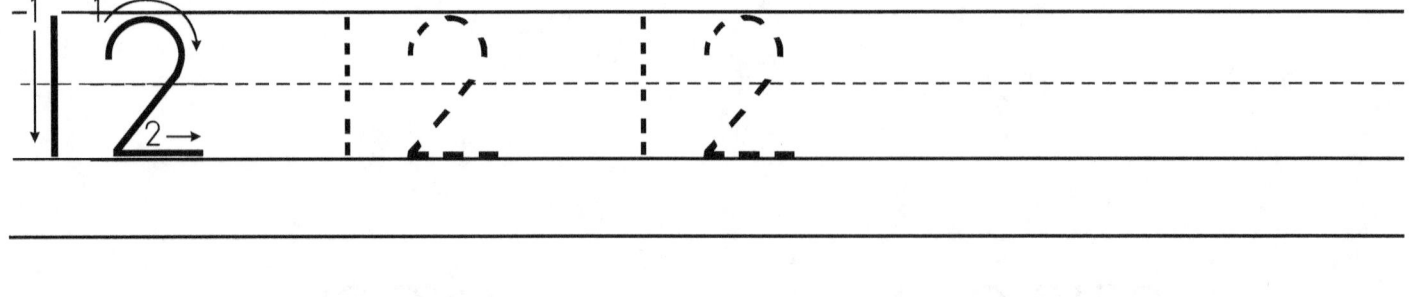

Trace the number name. Then write some on your own.

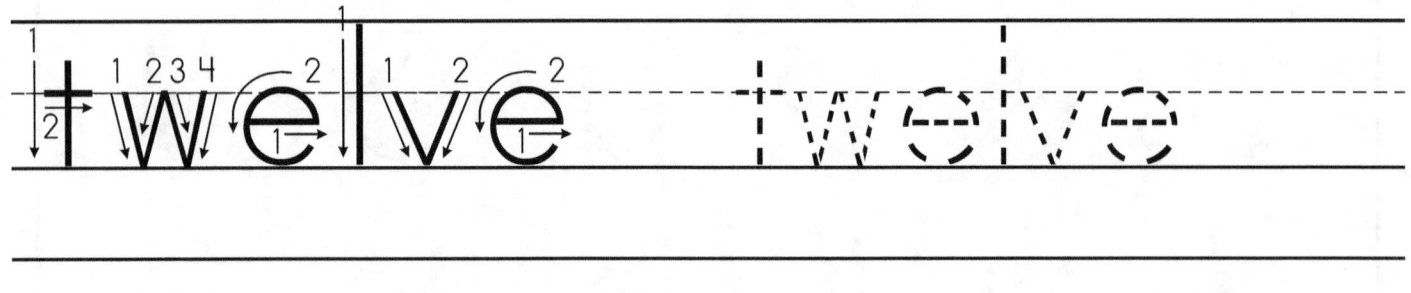

32 Bible Math: 1-2-3 Activity Sheets

Quail Publishers L.L.C

Name _____

Trace the numbers. Then write some on your own.

Draw **2** more squares. Then count how many squares there are in all.

☐ ☐ ☐ ☐ ☐ ☐ ☐ ☐ ☐ ☐

There are _____ squares.

Count the **almonds**. Then place circles around **12** of them.

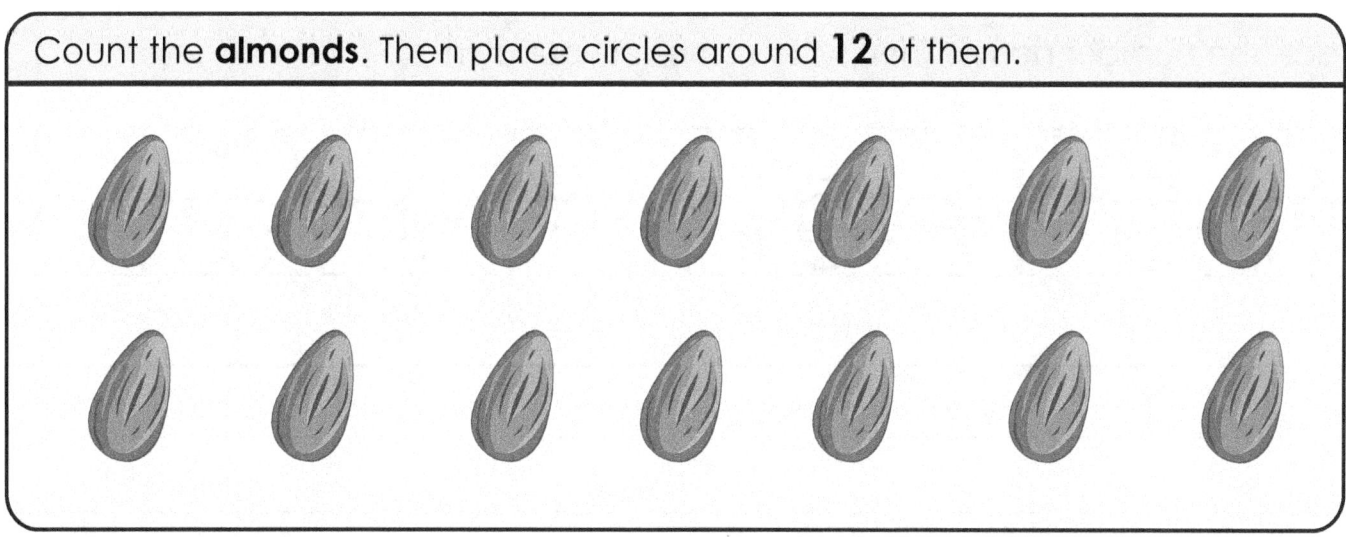

Quail Publishers L.L.C   Bible Math: 1-2-3 Activity Sheets 33

Name _____

Trace the numbers. Then write some on your own.

13 13 13 _____

_____

_____

Trace the number name. Then write some on your own.

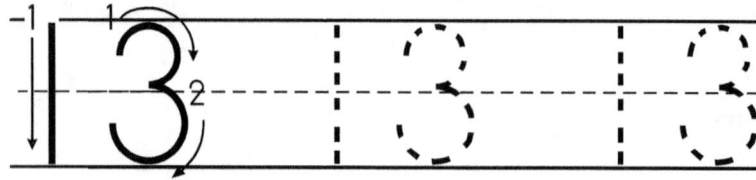

_____

_____

34 Bible Math: 1-2-3 Activity Sheets   Quail Publishers L.L.C

Name _____

Trace the numbers. Then write some on your own.

13 13 13

- -

Draw **3** more triangles. Then count how many triangles there are in all.

There are _____ triangles.

Count the **camels**. Then place circles around **13** of them.

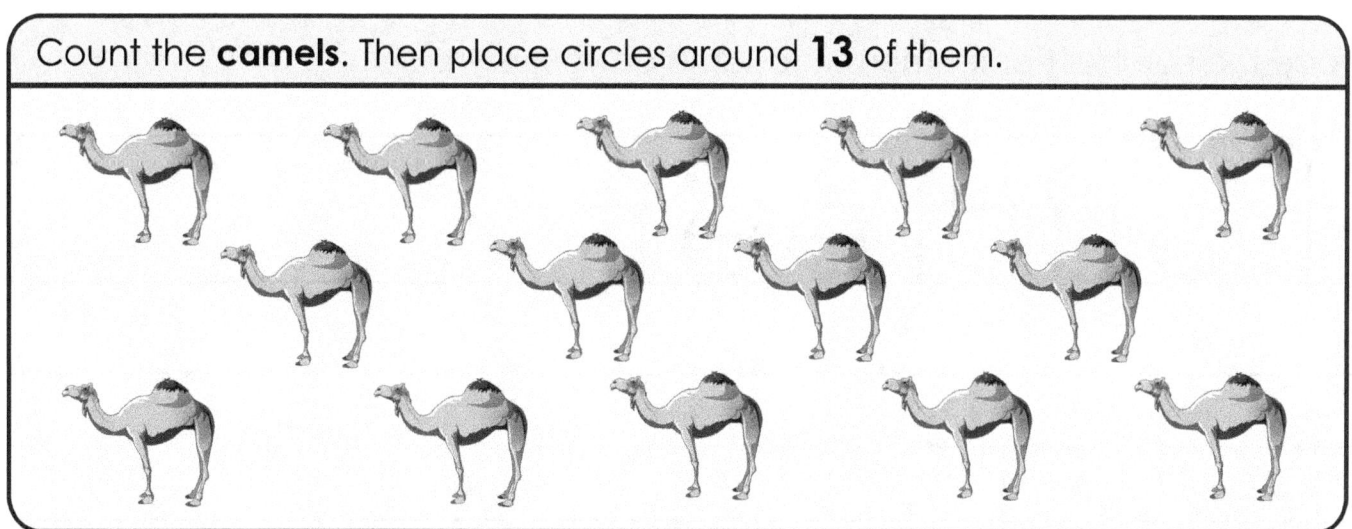

Quail Publishers L.L.C

Bible Math: 1-2-3 Activity Sheets 35

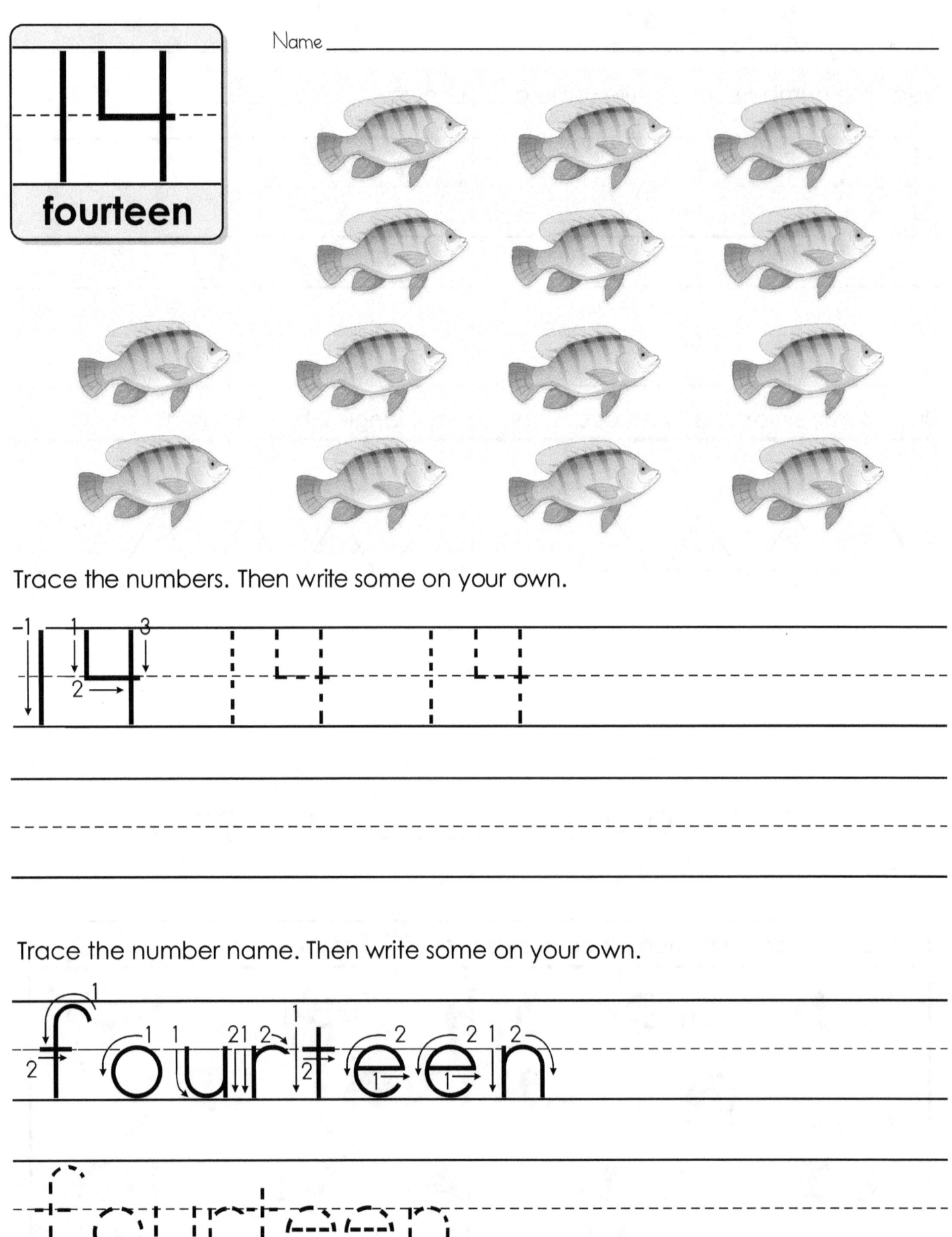

Trace the numbers. Then write some on your own.

Trace the number name. Then write some on your own.

Name _____

Trace the numbers. Then write some on your own.

Draw **4** more rectangles. Then count how many rectangles there are in all.

☐ ☐ ☐ ☐ ☐ ☐ ☐ ☐ ☐ ☐

There are _____ rectangles.

Count the **fish**. Then place circles around **14** of them.

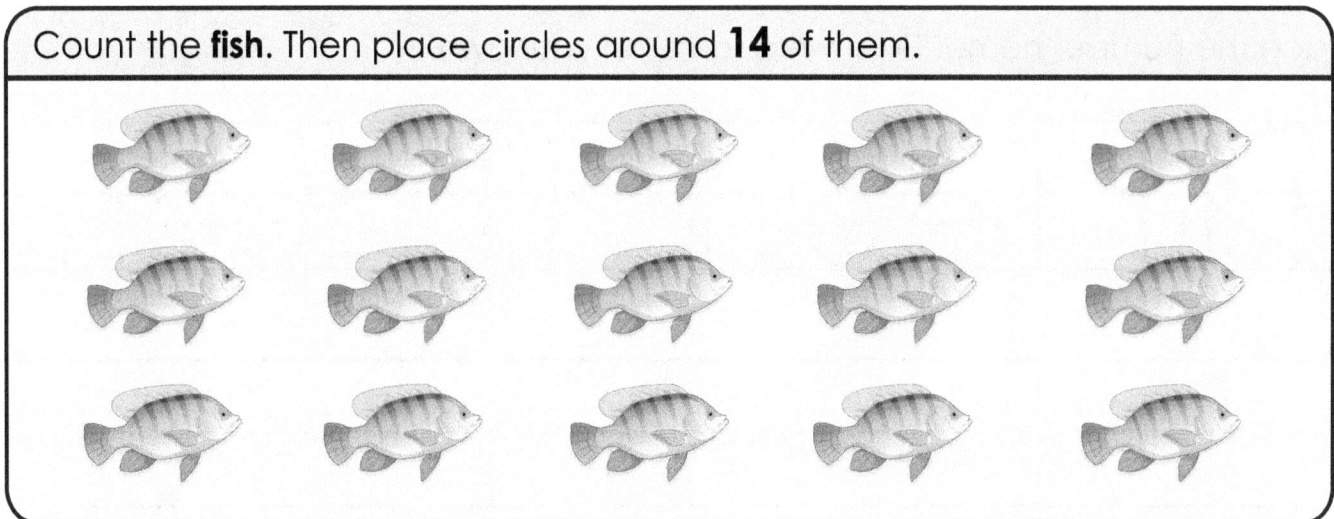

Quail Publishers L.L.C   Bible Math: 1-2-3 Activity Sheets

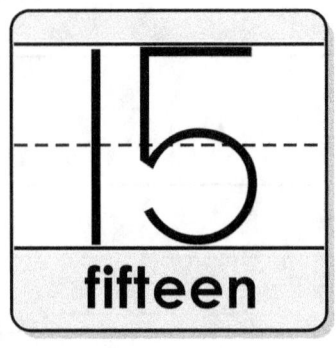

Name _____

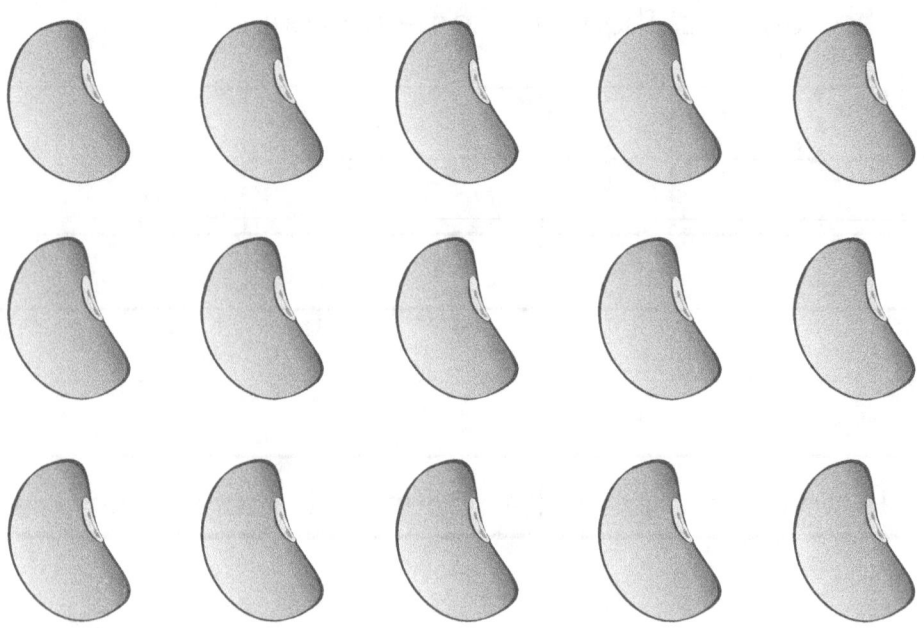

Trace the numbers. Then write some on your own.

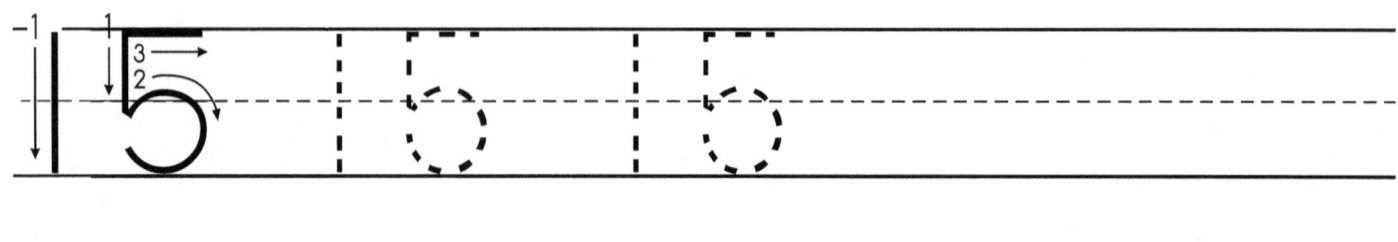

Trace the number name. Then write some on your own.

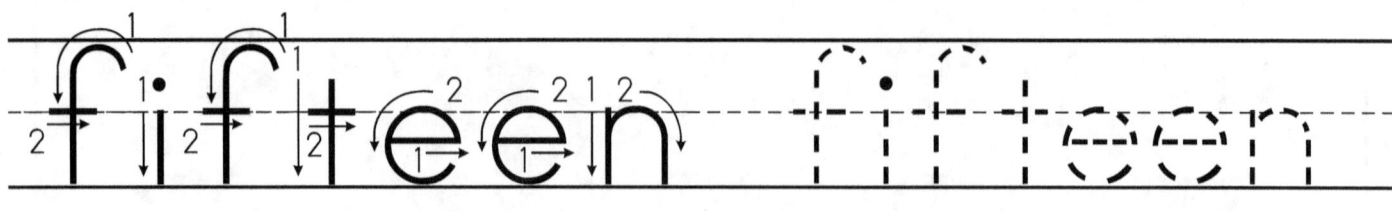

Name _____

Trace the numbers. Then write some on your own.

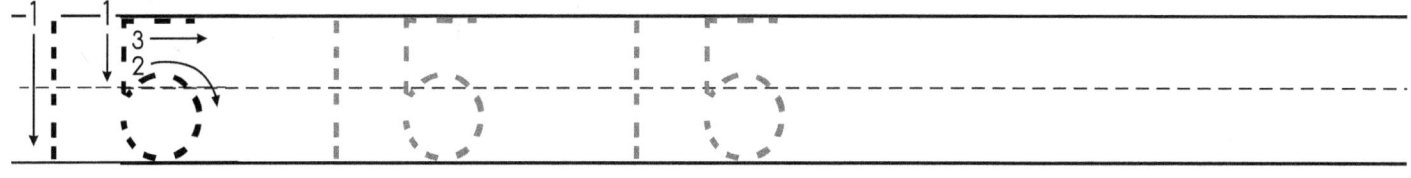

Draw **5** more ovals. Then count how many ovals there are in all.

There are _____ ovals.

Count the **beans**. Then place circles around **15** of them.

Quail Publishers L.L.C

Name _____

16
sixteen

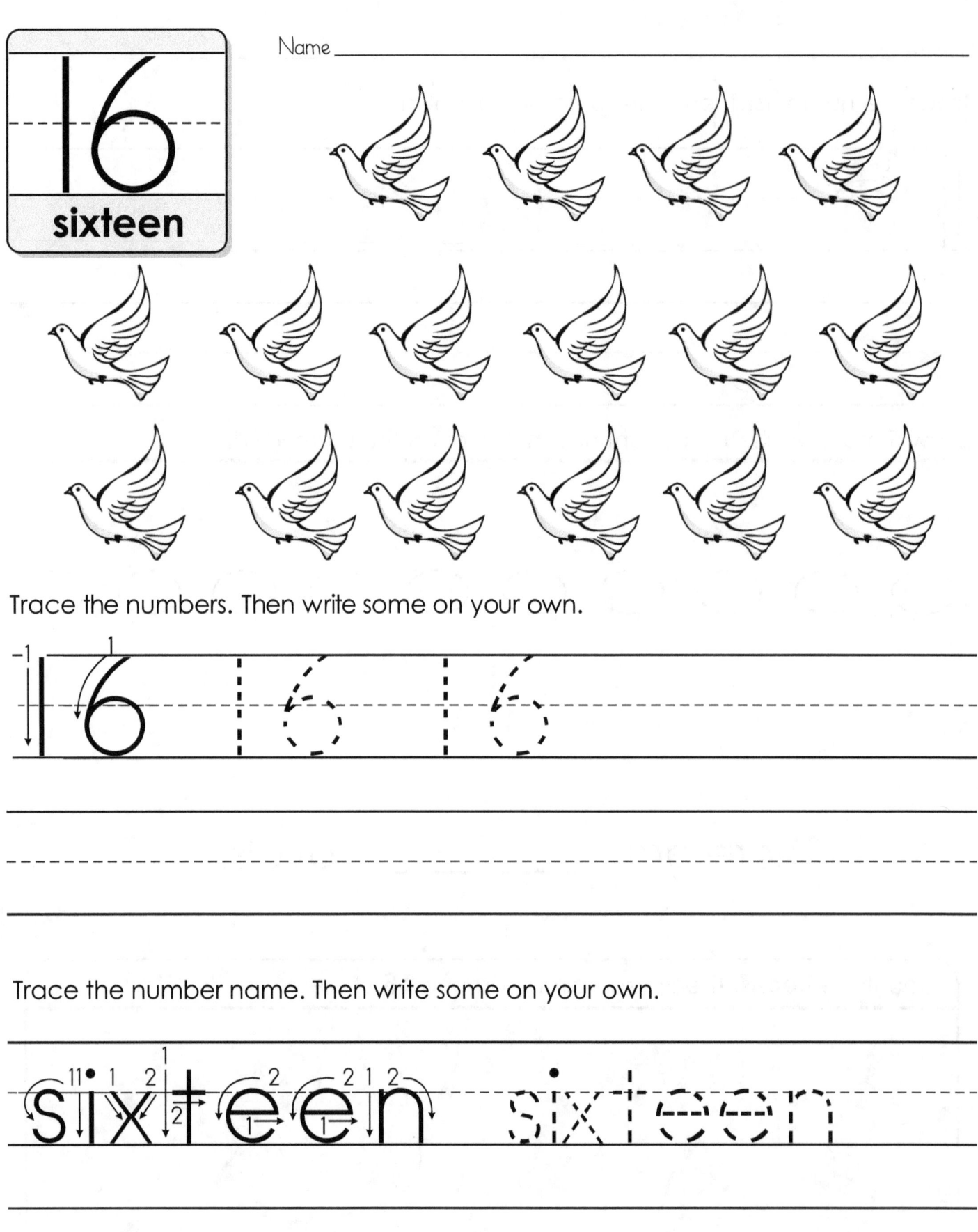

Trace the numbers. Then write some on your own.

16 16 16

Trace the number name. Then write some on your own.

sixteen sixteen

40 Bible Math: 1-2-3 Activity Sheets

Quail Publishers L.L.C

Name _____

Trace the numbers. Then write some on your own.

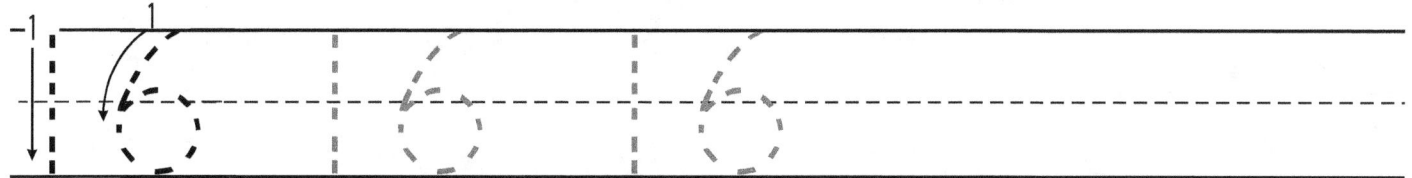

Draw **6** more diamonds. Then count how many diamonds there are in all.

There are _____ diamonds.

Count the **doves**. Then place circles around **16** of them.

Name _____

17
seventeen

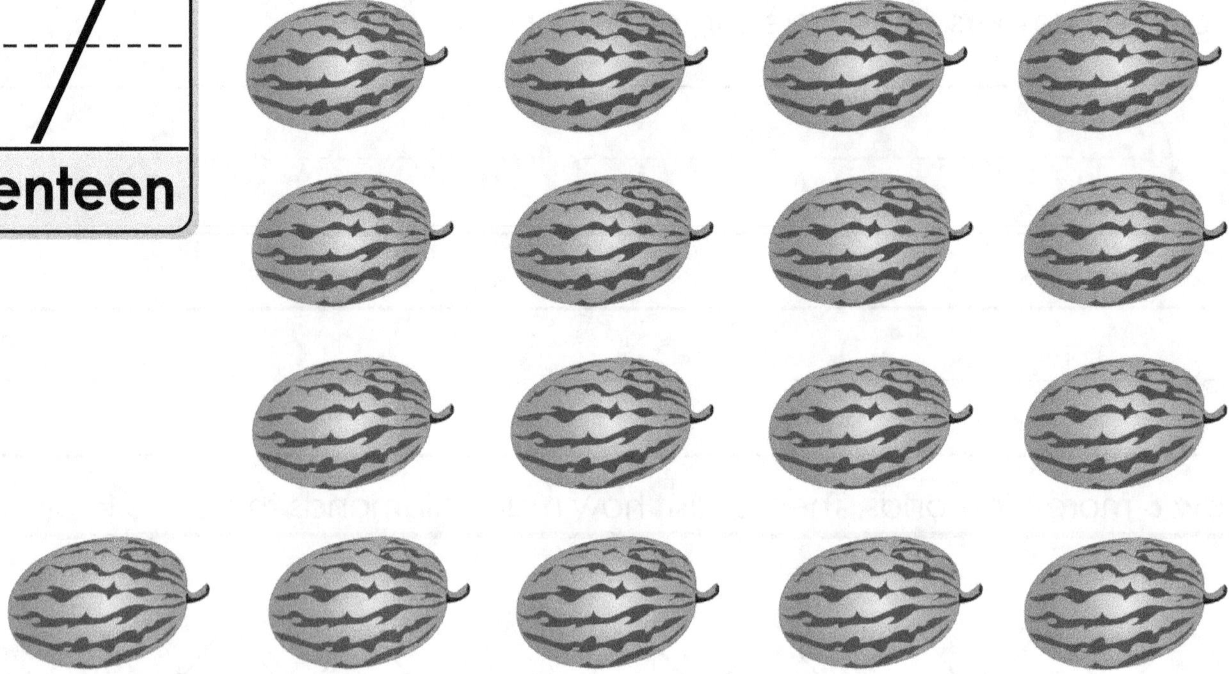

Trace the numbers. Then write some on your own.

17 17 17

Trace the number name. Then write some on your own.

seventeen

seventeen

Name _____

Trace the numbers. Then write some on your own.

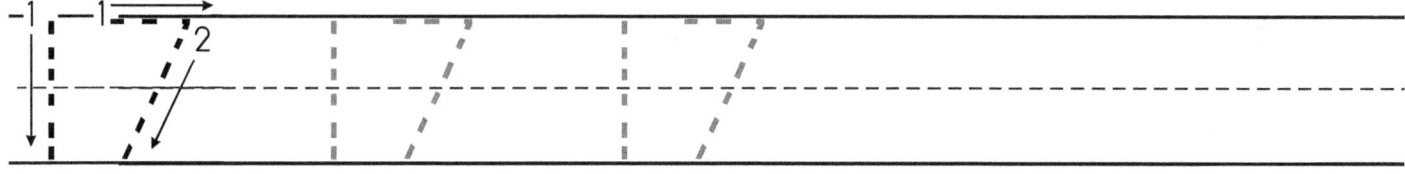

Draw **7** more pentagons. Then count how many pentagons there are in all.

There are _____ pentagons.

Count the slices of **melon**. Then place circles around **17** of them.

Quail Publishers L.L.C

Name _____

18
eighteen

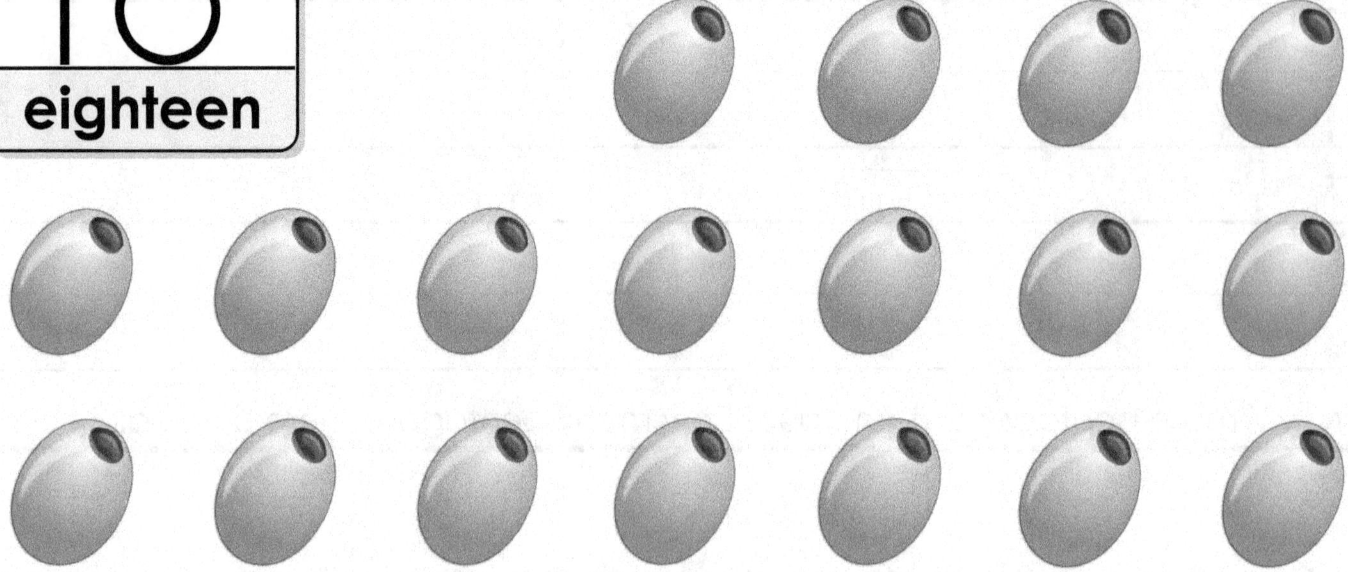

Trace the numbers. Then write some on your own.

18 18 18

Trace the number name. Then write some on your own.

eighteen

eighteen

Bible Math: 1-2-3 Activity Sheets

Quail Publishers L.L.C

Name _____

Trace the numbers. Then write some on your own.

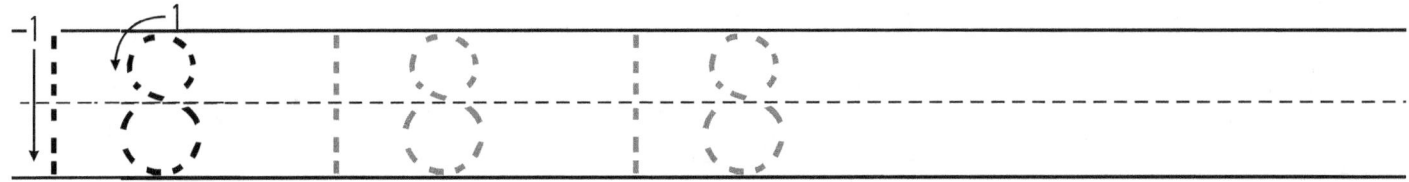

Draw **8** more hearts. Then count how many hearts there are in all.

There are _____ hearts.

Count the **olives**. Then place circles around **18** of them.

Quail Publishers L.L.C   Bible Math: 1-2-3 Activity Sheets

Name _____

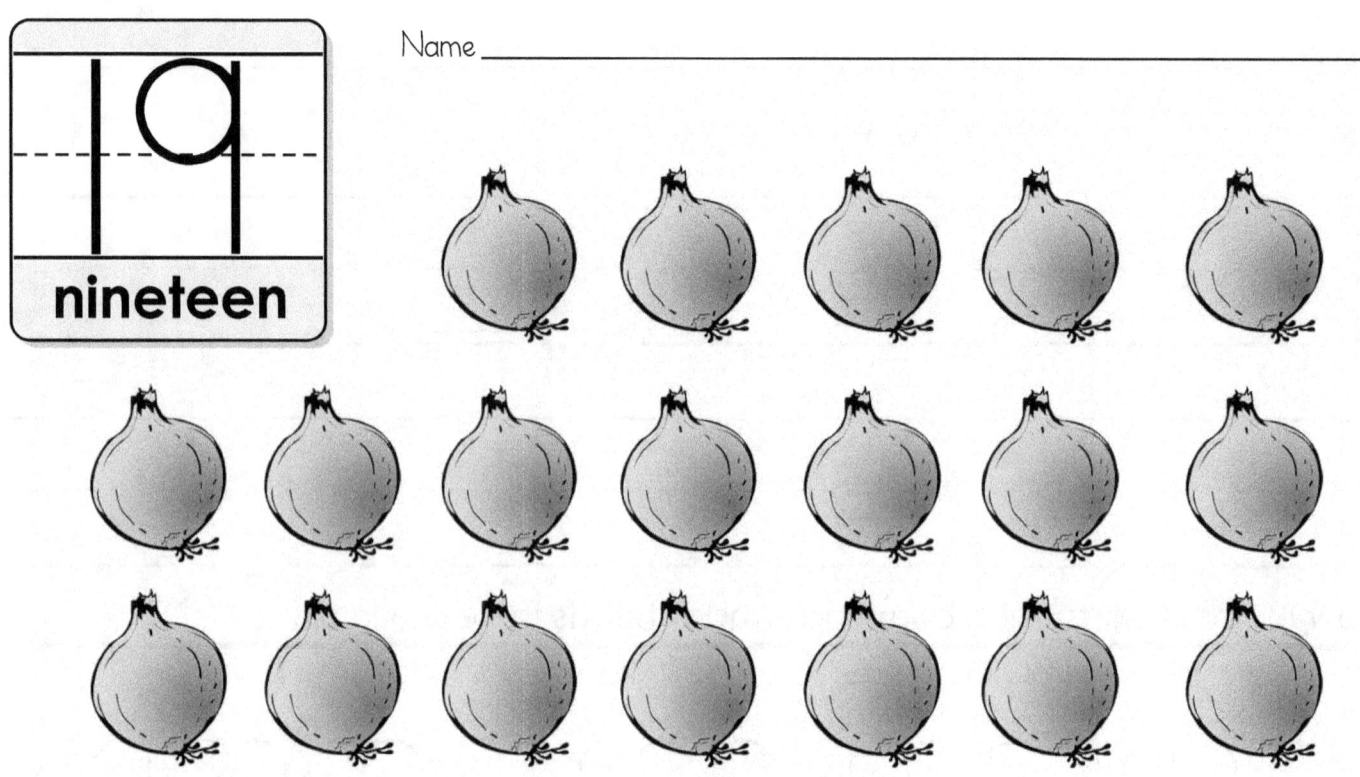

Trace the numbers. Then write some on your own.

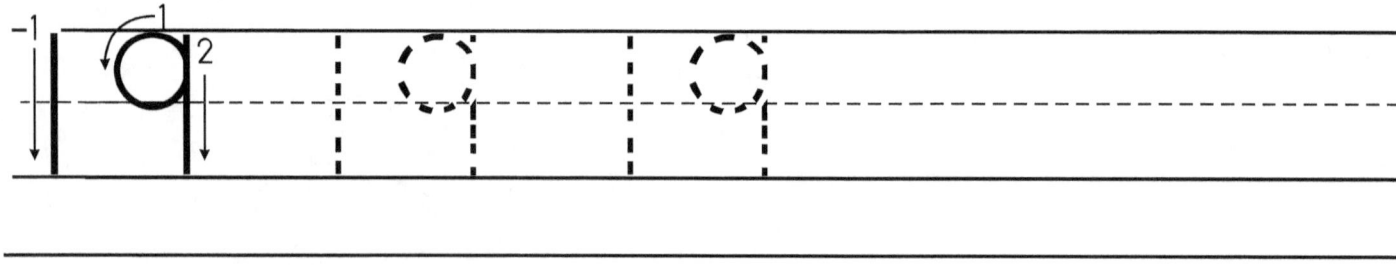

Trace the number name. Then write some on your own.

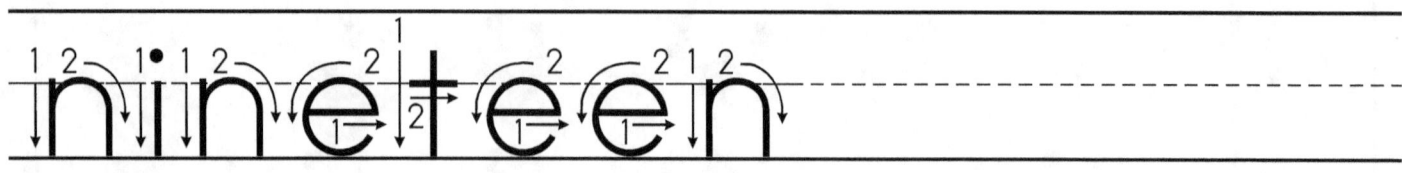

Name _____

Trace the numbers. Then write some on your own.

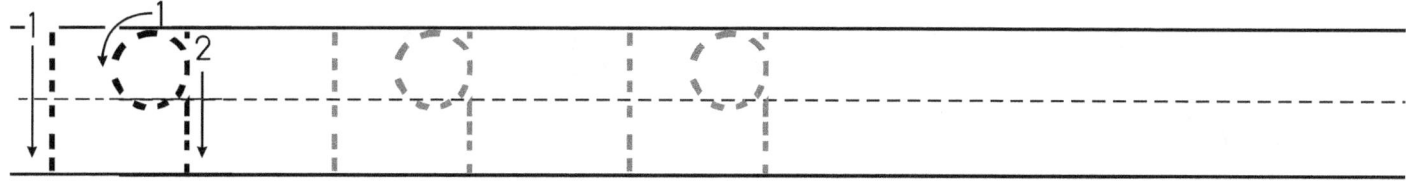

Draw **9** more crescents. Then count how many crescents there are in all.

There are _____ crescents.

Count the **onions**. Then place circles around **19** of them.

Quail Publishers L.L.C

Bible Math:1-2-3 Activity Sheets 47

Name _____

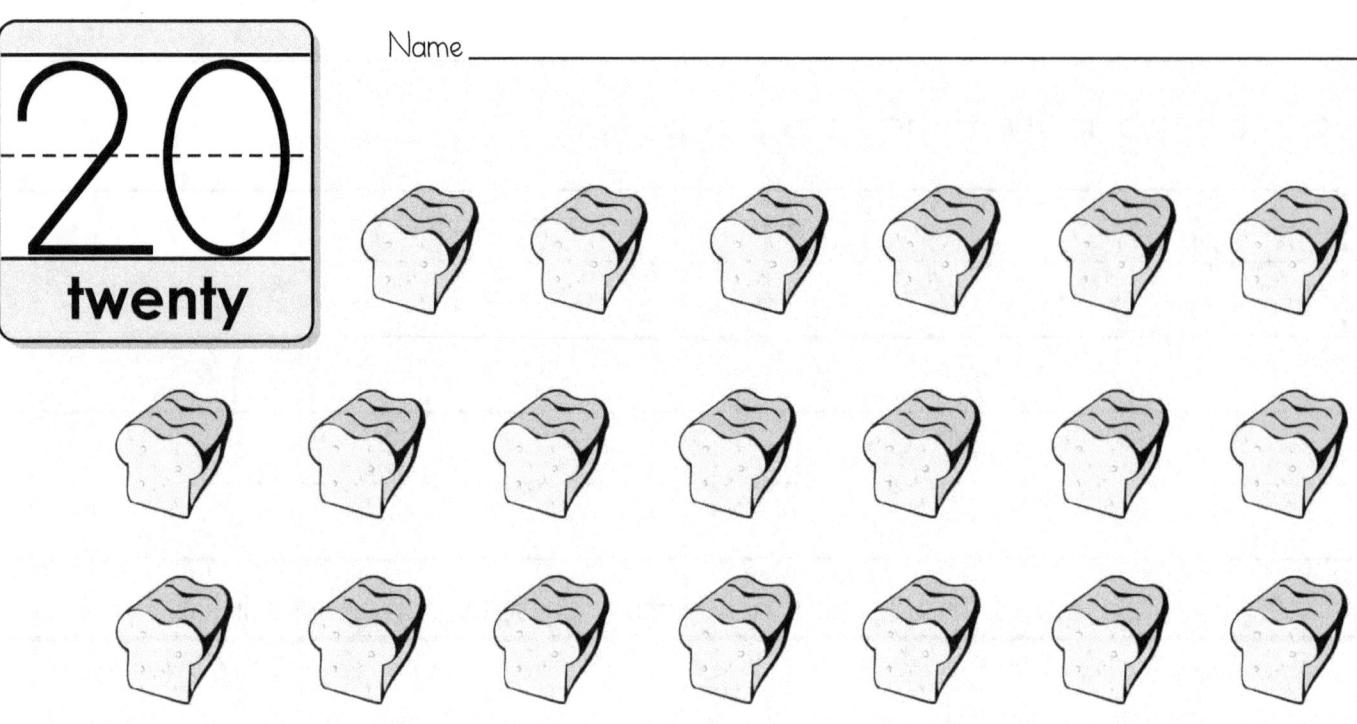

Trace the numbers. Then write some on your own.

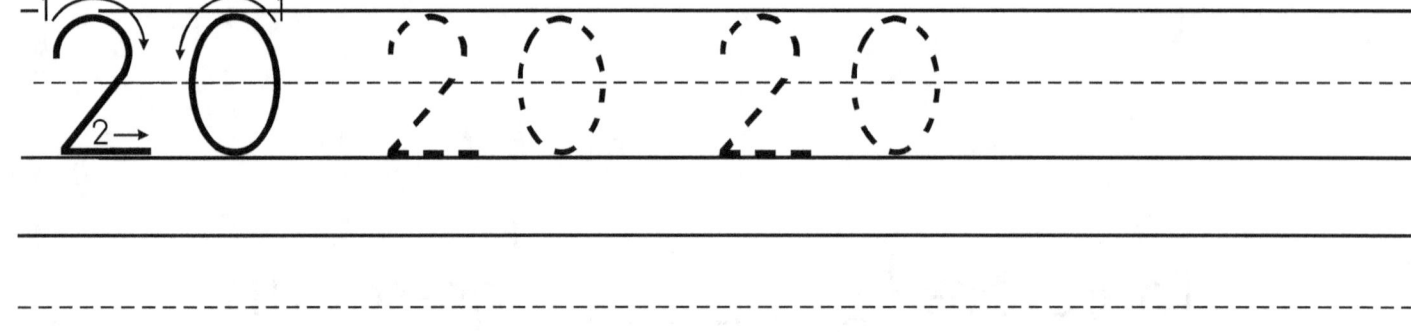

Trace the number name. Then write some on your own.

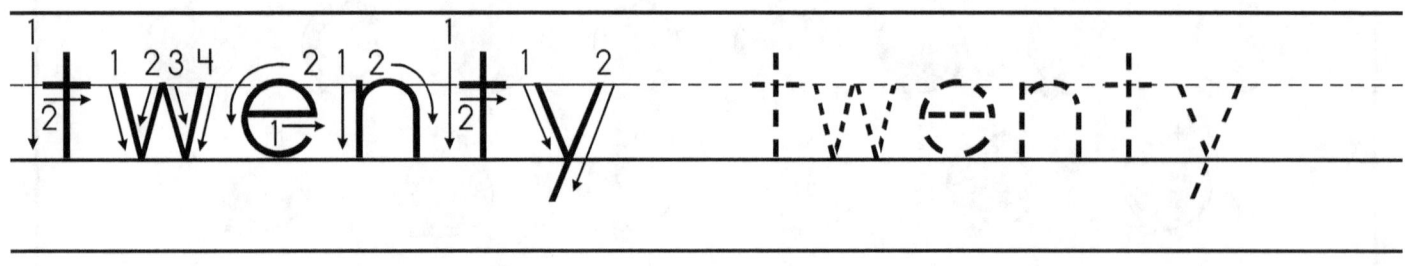

Name _____

Trace the numbers. Then write some on your own.

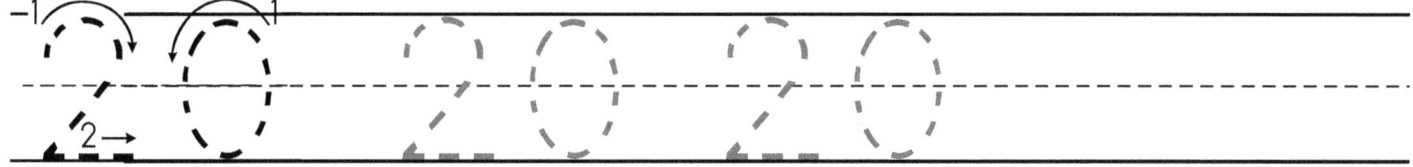

Draw **10** more semi-circles. Then count how many semi-circles there are in all.

There are _____ semi-circles.

Count the **loaves**. Then place circles around **20** of them.

Quail Publishers L.L.C

Bible Math: 1-2-3 Activity Sheets 49

Name_____

Draw a line to match the numbers to the correct groups.

11

12

13

14

15

16

17

18

19

20

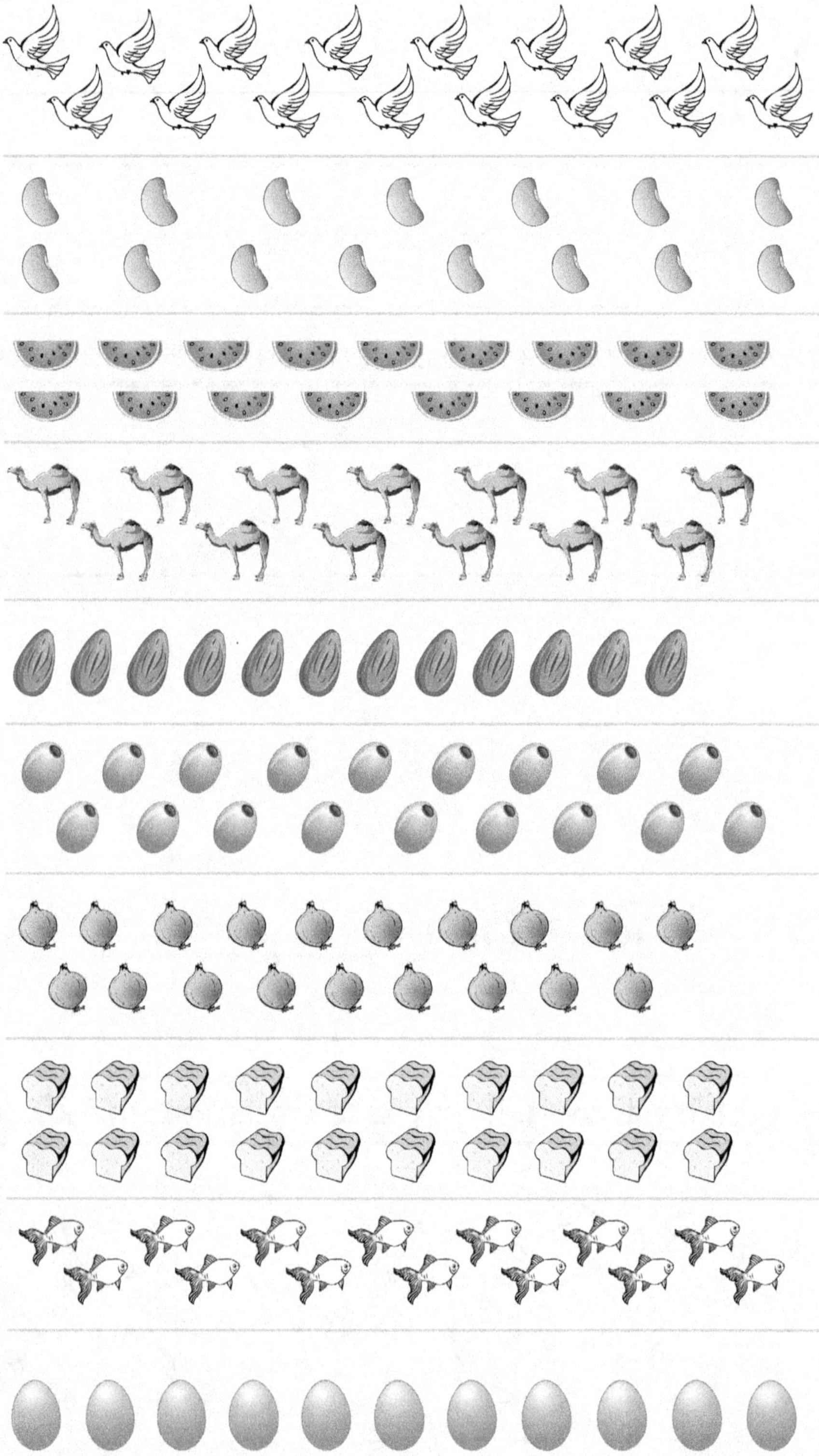

Name_____

Circle the numbers that represent the number names.

Eleven	10	11	19	1
Twelve	12	15	2	14
Thirteen	19	3	13	15
Fourteen	4	12	14	6
Fifteen	13	15	5	20
Sixteen	19	16	18	6
Seventeen	18	7	17	15
Eighteen	9	10	8	18
Nineteen	6	19	16	15
Twenty	0	10	20	2

Write the missing numbers in the empty spaces below to complete the table.

11		13		15
16		18		20

Write the correct number names in the empty spaces below to complete the table.

eleven		thirteen		fifteen
sixteen		eighteen		twenty

Quail Publishers L.L.C   Bible Math: 1-2-3 Activity Sheets

Name_____

ADDITION

When we add, we put things together. The plus or addition sign (+) is used to show that we are adding things. **Add** the following groups.

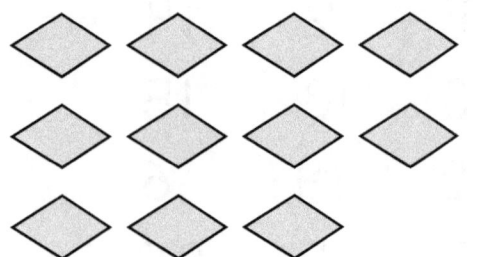 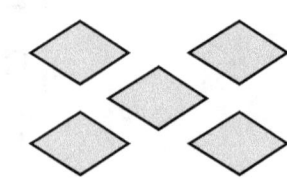

11   +   5   =   16

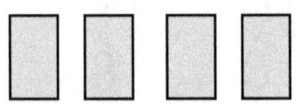 
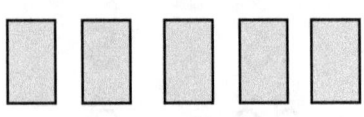 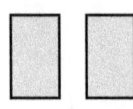
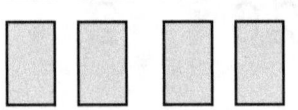 

13   +   6   =

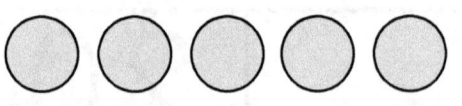 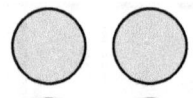
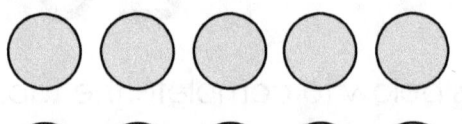 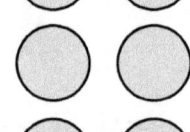
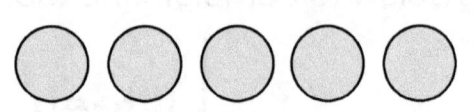 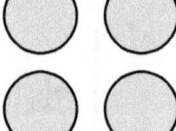

15   +   8   =

Name_____

ADDITION

Add the following groups.

17 + 3 =

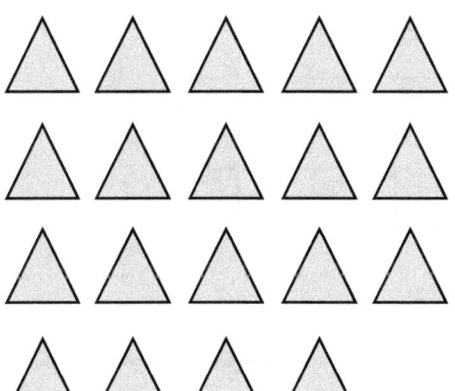 

19 + 9 =

SUBTRACTION

When we subtract, we take things away from a group. The minus or subtraction sign (−) is used to show that we are doing subtraction. Cross out the objects to show that you are **subtracting** and to help you to get the answer.

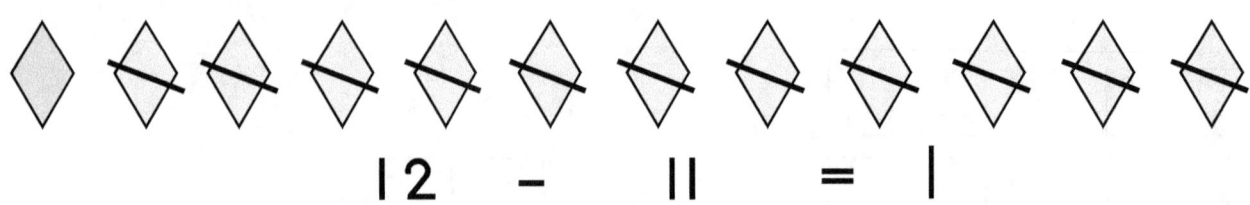

12 − 11 = 1

14 − 13 =

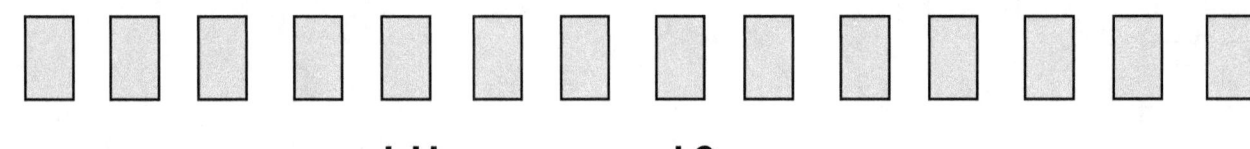

17 − 8 =

18 − 8 =

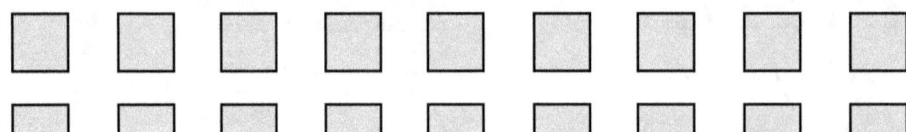

20 − 10 =

Name _____

REVISION

Place the missing numbers in the boxes below to complete the table.

1									10
	12							19	
		23					28		
			34			37			
				45	46				
				55	56				
			64			67			
		73					78		
	82							89	
91									100

www.ingramcontent.com/pod-product-compliance
Lightning Source LLC
Chambersburg PA
CBHW060530010526
44110CB00052B/2559